ARMS OF LIGHT

ARMS OF LIGHT

Selected First Poems

CLAIRE McALLISTER

New York: Alfred · A · Knopf   1964

ACKNOWLEDGMENTS

A number of these poems appeared originally in *The Atlantic Monthly*, *Botteghe Oscure*, *The Commonweal*, *The Critic*, *Envoy* (Dublin), *Jubilee*, *The Kenyon Review*, *The Literary Review*, *The Massachusetts Review*, *The Month*, *The New Pocket Anthology of American Verse*, *New Poems 1954*, a P.E.N. Anthology, *New World Writing*, *Partisan Review*, *Pax*, *Poetry*, *Poetry Ireland*, *Poetry London–New York*, *Points* (Paris), *Prairie Schooner*

L. C. catalog card number: 64–17707

This is a BORZOI BOOK, *published by* ALFRED A. KNOPF, INC. *Copyright © 1955, 1956, 1957, 1959, 1960, 1961, 1962, 1964 by Claire McAllister.*

FIRST EDITION

For my parents, Thomas and Dorothy McAllister

CONTENTS

I   *DISARMED*

⚘ A PANTOUM FOR MORNING[1]

*. . . so doth feare insinuate itself into every action
and passion of the mind.*   JOHN DONNE

Morning pours a cold flame through the curtains;
We, O my dreams, are caught as fire takes the spread.
In silk light dressed to pose her questions
Mute, the Morning sits upon the bed.

We, O my dreams, are caught as fire takes the spread;
She is there, a hard bright challenge in our eyes.
Mute, the Morning sits upon the bed.
We fear to draw and fear not to draw the blinds.

She is there, a hard bright challenge in our eyes.
It were better, perhaps, to be sprightly like boys deaf to danger.
We fear to draw and fear not to draw the blinds.
It were better as we bury the head, this were sloth and not fear.

It were better, perhaps, to be sprightly like boys deaf to danger.
In the cloak of the sheets we hide seeking safety in dreaming.
It were better as we bury our heads, this were sloth and not fear.
We try for a while to forget we've no answers for Morning.

In the cloak of the sheets we hide, seeking safety in dreaming
While Morning pours a cold flame through the curtains.
We try for a while to forget we've no answers for Morning
In silk light dressed to pose her questions.

1. *Pantoum* is an ancient French verse form.

DARK NIGHT

Desperation comes
Picking at the beat of the heart
Like a crow when the twilight meadow
Is his bare orange target.

Desperation comes
And I am limp like the scarecrow
Who can no more deceive
The sharp yellow beaks;

The rags upon it useless
And absurd in their vain purpose
Like the distractions I conjure
When the end of every means is to scare

Desperation; or it may come
Gently first, a tame lion
Licking the lonely hand and
Consoling as slowly he draws the blood

In time to the surface of the skin
When he springs to consume.
Desperation claims its own
If they let it, the dejected, the alone.

Could I bring you where the red west falls
Into the hemlocks, far from any road,
When gunshot rips the wind and evil tales
Are hinted at when a disgruntled toad
Croaks out at that orange of a moon,
Then might the night not hunt you.
                        One was spared
When through the lonely hut of Daniel Boone
A mountain-lion sprang and, crouching, stared;
Until the nerve of either one should break
Each stared at each; it was the cat that crept
Away.
      O love, I say: let us look straight
At this terror in the heart that one day leapt
And crouches at us; and, as coldly, stare.
Why should we have the nerve-strings of a hare?

THE LAURELS ARE CUT

Nous n'irons plus aux bois;
Les lauriers sont coupés . . .

Wild red raspberry staining my hand like a murder,
Down by the Delaware River my eyes and my arms
Ached with the weight of all the wild fruits and flowers
I left ungathered, and to gamble for trinkets and charms!
    To the woods we'll go no more; they have chopped the laurel;
    Hewed are the laurels, and the hinges rust on the barns.

In another country once, you too grew wise
Calling the wet mosses, creepers, all, by name.
And your words like wild-berries startle who sell and buy,
And you stare through the attic-bright windows streaked with old rain.
    But we'll go no more to the woods; the loved laurel cries;
    Hewed are the laurels, and wild red raspberries stain.

Fungi, foliage, fruit—you recall to us Eden;
Our clothes hang heavy, and sounds in the city streets
Like bank-robbers take from the mind that green money and its freedom;
Then sing how the laurels are cut, and no lamb bleats.
    To the woods we'll go no more; the laurel is kindling;
    Hewed are the laurels we knew when the world was sweet.

JULY IN THE JARDIN DES PLANTES

The summerdays moved with the pace of a caged lion;
To stroll through crowds by the parkgates at dusk was a game:
O could we snatch out of that dusk a moment
That memory might, like meat or whip-lash, tame.

To take what shape of cloud or smile was given
Was to stroll no longer the lost one's eyes
Upon us except obliquely, the way next autumn,
Last spring were peering at summer as through bars.

Mist rising up from the morning-warmed grass was a spectre
Muffling the noise of the nurses and nursed by the sand.
Sycamore-branches stuck outside the nightmare;
I traced them like the lines in the palm of my hand

Thinking someday under a sycamore I shall watch summers
Remembering with pride, with shame, the streets of youth,
The cities that hummed with the din of their ruined lovers,
Traffic-lights that shattered the dreaming dusk.

Truth that we look for in lilacs each spring changes color
When love is but a longing for something not said.
Often the telling of dreams is the great error:
The dream like a perfect crime must remain in the head.

And as the pace of summer quickened I thought of what hovered
Outside its unthinking joys till I knew that the knot,
The knots in dreams haven't come from defeat, but desire;
It is not within nightmares we walk alone, but without.

Sun hung high in the yellow six o'clock darkness;
Motorcars and crowds swam in that light.
We still had the rest of July and all of August . . .
But the summerdusk darkens; lo, leaves turn red overnight!

Someone had to write it out that way,
With the logic of a calculating thief
Who turns the diamond over till his eye
Be blear and, bit by bit, his bold heart shrink.

There is where he wandered,
Sorting out his thoughts
   And we forget the squandered
Years before he caught
   The shadow in his mural,
The highlight in his verse,
   Or the sinew in his sculpture—
The sacred, secret Word:
      On you he turned, O Laurel
      Leaves: your crown he cursed.

Rome

II   *ARMS OF LIGHT*

A DEDICATION

For Father D'Arcy

Lalage, saved from shipwreck on the seas,
Dedicates to those who bade her live—
The ocean deities—
Her wringing hair; there's nothing else to give.

Dedicates to those who bade her live
And told her walk on the tall waves with pride,
Her wringing hair; there's nothing else to give
Except the hoar sea-fruit at her side.

Walk out over the black waves with pride.
No sea was ever crossed not crossed in fear.
Her heart that talked to men died;
Who but the sea-gods hear?

No sea was crossed not crossed in fear.
From a land of slime and shard she gives what is left.
Then may blind love see, so brought ashore,
And she beg, wringing out her hair: Accept!

What from all the flotsam had she kept?
Forgetting salt-stung eyes and tired arms,
She entreats: My seaweed hair, accept.
He goes his way, with fishing-nets and psalms.

Stung eyes, tired arms,
The dark divinities
Go their way, with fishing-nets, and psalms
Plucking lovers from shipwreck on the seas.

Bold charms, the broken arms of Aphrodite—:
Behold how close the soul of man they clasp.
The sockets in your head are blank, Athene—:
Cold goddess eyes struck blind when Paul walked past.

  Faraway in the long-ago
The moon climbed down when they came—
With aloes and spices they came.
(What are surnameable loves to me?)
The moon that rolls like the stone to the tomb,
If eyes look to see, rolls it open at dawn.
They came with aloes and spices they came.
  He is risen. He is not here. O say
  Is that You? Or only a pillar of sun?

O you who are derisive of the drama
Dared to be believed in by a few
Who in their wild aloneness came on the manna
Sent for the one song, the sorrows they knew,
Be wary with derision for you trample
Only your own lilies in the dark,
    Lilies that at night all radiance throw,
    The lilies that for Easter risings grow!

DAPHNE

From a hillslope I look on the wet fields flattening before me,
Mud holding mirrors, and the withered twigs alive with rain;
I would pick my way through the darkness and straining bramble
But I'd only be stumbling to that weather-rank tomb, my name—

A name never meant for men's mouths, that to no man I'd answer.
And what path would I step but the small way down my own ear?
Since the day that I fled them along the fields of my pride
Every tree says, Stand, tall in your silence, till blood return from fear.

But if I stand so, I feel my human limbs taking root
And the glint on the ground from a lichened twig might stare me blind,
And the Apollo of my Imagination pursuing—his arms, O his arms almost
        about me—
Would he leave me there forever, with my love branching stiff from the spine?

Yet a form has walked in the broken sun of the wood,
Has hunted with the arrows of prayer where the feared boar drips red.
Him let me see! if mistaking but a birch for his gesture:
Those hands could change my sad flesh which change to Body the bread.

Or the terrible secret, is it lodged in the rings of a tree?
That I, slowed as Laurel, had else ambled wilder than most
Did I not know He walked, the Christ, sounding all depths from his eyes,
Cry, Why should he so please my soul? Half blessed is half cursed.

That it's out of the corner of my eye, only, dare I now look.
To have followed a love to its lonely throne in the wood
Sees me struck clutching earth, slow leaves of my brain brought to light,
Speechless with rustling: God is now Body and Blood.

If the rude wood I rambled were my own empty loving, he pitied.
Lord, among these leaves, now, let Your sun toss a few coins.
See a thing stilled staring into distances reflecting You in his eyes;
Lord unless You breathe through me now, let bark shroud my loins . . .

LOCUSTS IN THE WILDS

. . . their right hand is filled with gifts. PSALM XXV

In their right hands are ropes of pearls, ropes to strangle you, child.
They would take you smiling away; they would dry the tears' springs;
The left hand leading to banquets of kings, not the King's . . .
Starve so! child; or feast as did he finding locusts in the wilds.

The wines in their goblets are those of the first crushed grapes.
They would hold you tall toasts—stretch of arm that makes all the ropes ease.
Child, their kisses would crown you with myrtle, their praise be Spring's green.
And the hand that would crown you so, crowns you a slave, less than slave.

But as, outcast, the wheel of night turns and your dreams test its rack,
Your lone loving like a leper approaching, by yourself unloved,
See a moment what stands in garment by no hand spun;
Sight a moment what Dante's eyes loved, and all Sad becomes Glad.

Wet winds travelled spitting petals at the windows as I wakened,
Gladdened by clouds become buffaloes whitening in rampage.
Nerve winding high, by the sinews of a breeze I was taken,
Plucked from the pillows to a place in those clouds, lonely-happy
Feeling sadness through my limbs as saplings in rain strain to growth.
O all brightness come posting on black prayer, it came as the boughs
Moaned sweet the morning before anxiety woke.
As the dark pines stretched to the wind, I stretched toward the Spouse,
Walked out, picking mint by a brook, clutching misers' gold.

And Lord, though I spoke not your name, did you know this were praying?
If pagan, and proud, thinking my findings found the mint sweet?
Currants I crushed tricked me there—O lost wine of the veins!
And the tang in my head told me cry: Let my hair dry those feet.
And as staring I stood there, stilled by a stone that bled,
For a moment the brain was crystal, swept of its ashes,
Ashes the lack of you sprinkled till thinking were dead.
To have turned . . . but your cup was the sun, burning hard at my back
And the Host, the hole in the sky, the full moon numbing head.

But your light breaking frail through the mint-leaves . . . to look, then, I dared;
Fern on the banks tossing mist told of seraphs on earth
And the mist that was drifting strands of a saint's shorn hair—
Though if mention were made you were near, I'd have turned on the words.
Through slats in a hayloft, later, a pale arm of sun
Washed gold the straw, sent stalks dipping points through to heavens:
A barnful of sceptres! And I stretched forth that day to have come
To this morning that says you were closer for prayers not said
Like any true lover who hears what his love has stirred dumb.

The oranges were gold; the myrrh was crushed pine;
With applewood, frankincense burnt sweet the air.
On that night of His birth we stepped out of time,
The skies held with wonder as ever they were.

On the mistletoe-sprig a saint had hung tears.
On Twelfth Night I'll cry: Leave me the fruits of the Feast!
Shall the world walk on as if no song were heard?
Sweet Lord, let me follow Your star down my breast!

Or the darkling mistletoe stares my heart chill.
Let me recall, when snows become rain,
A carol that told of valleys filled,
Of hills brought low, and the rough ways, plain.

Young, I had seen His star, come with gifts,
With honeycombs, walnuts, lemonleaves, plums . . .
And the thrust of nostalgia pierces—and twists;
Then bleed: for such rubies and rags He comes.

Stable-door, open! Camel, cow, sheep,
Could your round eyes, reflecting, but bend on me here,
The dew in my head goes, the firelights leap:
Through the crack in the brain shines the hay-bright manger.

May the heart look this night past the depths of its debt,
With carols, spices, sparkling grates,
Walk to the courts of the Lord, guided yet
By a star on a stable we have loved, loved too late.

When the milk-white Lamb lies bathed in blood,
When pinetrees smoulder and the gold is rind,
We who had carolled for joy must weep:
He comes making bright the dark hollows of the mind.

III *ARMS OF LOVE*

ILION IN GOTHAM

For Conor

No. Mitchell Place was never windier than when
It blew your wit into her ears, tricked tears,
Strewed loose the locks she'd for Love's bier have sheared;
There drew with you not cabs, but charioteers
    Drove down the storied streets of Ilion.
    No, Mitchell Place was windier never than then.

East Riverwinds wove Delphic spells not till
Your eyes were Dardanelles dared folly dive.
(Not dare is die.) Yet she'd not prise that eye:
You'd trap her wild grief, bring back gay alive,
    Would comb the tangled mane of lion will,
    Send hectic strands of dreaming sleek as silk;

Whose vision wreathed the garlands for her shoulder;
And though she'd laid them on the King's cold tomb,
Red grapes the gods had ripened for her truth
You gathered—and Anacreon winged her youth:
    The topless towers of Gotham rising golder:
    Lamps of Ilion! still each window smoulders . . .

So know no marble heart beat in that breast,
Though cool as her north dunes the empty hand;
It's that the vanished arms of Venus cracked
When they the Flesh of Light in a stable's trough grasped.
    Embrace her though her arms are all but cleft:
    The broken arms of Light do fold Love best.

I

Perseus you were. Or Pericles? Who was I?
That down my skies should flock the wings each asks,
That from my skies should fly the cawing black;
And then this riddle: your gaze on the sands
Of my gold hours, spreading like the Sphinx—
Your gaze on my most best of memoried lands
Knows answers all: why something like the flight
Of swallow south, or from his splendid drink
Anacreon to his lyre, or to his height
The mountain climber goes—some wing in the night
     Has turned us gay where most we could be sad.

II

A wingèd-chariot took me through that town,
Where 49th Street crossed its fingers, cars
That once drove Agamemnon through the dawn
Were hailed: you walked as one triumphant to the wars.

From tower windows Troy I saw: smoke-wreaths
Choked dreams, but Homer's history was being made.
Your wit was every leaf that would renew the year with green.
Cauldrons all could bubble on: no witch would trick your brain.

III

Morose the moon at midnight mocks my tunes.
I hear my footsteps on the stones declare
This hand was only tearing at the looms,
Looms of useless song instead of hair.

Too late to tell you yours it was whose lilt
Built wingèd cars that carried me like wine
Whereby the blood I thought with might ink spill
To soothe the furious Muse and startle rhyme.

Yet anxious for the oracle of you,
Rhetorically I would describe the charm
But lions turn to kittens licking fur of rue:
I grope for words as once in streets your arm.

Seafarer, Seafarer, fare thee well then;
Fare thee far better on wine-darker waves;
The gods that were generous and sent you ashore
Shift like the winds and sail you away.

Seafarer, see me so tearing my looms:
Not silk-threads but song-ends. My swan song, prepare:
Sing the song to end songs! I'd sung else had you stayed,
But the gods were against it: our day was too fair.

Seafarer, cease to seek dark roads beyond me!
No use; and your shadow shall block the sun's rays.
While we dance on the sands the gods plan our sadness
And I was too green for your high golden ways.

Nausicaä, smooth away sands, raze his footprint;
Bruise them and soothe you; he seeks darker truth.
Nausicaä, seek you another. Nausicaä
Sees but eclipse of her sun. Farewell, Moon.

Fare thee well, Seafarer; fare thee then well.
Fare thee far better in firmer embraces.
Return when the griefs of the gods are assuaged and
True sages wage war on the wisdoms that age us.

Fare thee well, Future, and Folly and Fanfare;
Fare thee well, Fantasy. Furrow dark field.
Return when of our loves the gods have had plenty,
For when the gods envy they steal.
   Return on a day the winds shift again quickly
   And I to your valor may yield.

Willowleaves that sweep the pond
Wept when fair Ophelia smiled,
When Desdemona grew too fond;
They weep for sweetest wits gone wild.

Weed-tangled floors I see beyond
Say, "Let no looking-glass beguile;
Search no man's eye if it grow fond:
Their deaths were dark, their eyes were mild,

Their songs . . . " O were they black, or bright?
I hear the beating of those wings—
Ophelia swims across the night
And Desdemona, combing, sings.

I'd hear you, love, but a cold wind stings;
The willows whisper, joy-exiled;
Hell-doors fly open, and they sing
Of boughs and herbs as would a child.

And now ripe scent of threshed alfalfa,
Of daisy, timothy, clover of June,
Strokes the air, it brings them nearer:
Fields are with their fragments strewn.

The June air growing colder, colder
Shuts my eyes, and still I see—
Smoothing the linen, Desdemona
Robes the night with willowleaves.

§

O blossoming beans, the glittering grain,
Honeysuckle softened breeze:
As close as April grass to rain,
I see them, sad as northern seas.

The blonde hair tangling, ever bright—
All flowering weeds are those she brings.
Ophelia swims across the night
And Desdemona, combing, sings.

§

I held your face, love; then they stepped
Beside you; then the willows touched
The throat to song, and singing yet,
Love wanders down, with willows clutched.

Indue me to that element,
To clear the throat, do gentle deeds,
Describe the day that was. Lament
Sings all the songs, colors the weeds.

Turn hell to favor with refrains,
Remembering how Ophelia flung
The tables upsidedown. The games
Are tricked. Tell me what gambler won.

Play on, to lose, but till the last
Let no ears hear what silence heard;
If they ask why the song is black,
Say a weeping-willow stirred.

J. C. W.

Much madness is divinest sense . . . EMILY DICKINSON

Not Palisades' gay plunge won as his laugh—
Sweep of those roller-coasters in his ribs,
Though brow and brown eye steer a Dark Night's ship—
Once navy's wars', now brain-waves'—not to kiss
    Life like the girl goodbye. Tall as at mast,
    He waves salute to tears, keeping Lent fast.

    Striding the kingdom's woods, cavalier, child-wild,
Though scourged by earthly rules that broke his youth.
Who climb their own high truths, struck down poor fool;
And whom the gods most love must sport their wounds.
    But limbs of grief, like the lions of March, spring mild—
    His eyes as warm as knew no day but smiled.

     §

It's in that voice I know how wars are won,
That hand as it picks up hopes like broken glass—
No step to bleed as yours. In prayer I task
My God: Whose gambler-throw tossed as to damn
    Your dreams? And then your wit locks thief-thoughts dumb.
    Then hoists my praise: I praise your untameable love.

It is not easy, clambering to intangible fruit,
And not the mule's carrot, gold, luring men less mad.
Heart, better far who stride Night's luckless lands, and
Know no hand dangling prize but his God's own hand.
    Then strider, wait for me; teach me the rules:
    To step as barefoot-free while in those boots
    No hell tore off, till Heaven were stormed! that muddy, golden boot
    Valor wore, till '*eviL*'-spelled-'*Live*', is on your foot.

✳ *OVID'S MULBERRY*[1]

His blood streamed to the tree,
Staining white fruit to red. METAMORPHOSIS, BOOK IV

Warm rains, and Octobers down shingles go sliding,
Down eaves cluttered deep with frames of springfruit
And under my head over pillow go riding
Remembered legends. I hear the outlawed hoof;

And then the mirrors—every roof
Silver with Thisbe's tears, and through the crevice
In my head: Take you care! while yet there is youth;
Mulberries in the raindarks are staining sight scarlet.

O lion-hearted love, but one single instant
Can twist our story to a fatal knot:
Remember the mulberries dripping, branch scarlet
With Pyramus' blood. To conclusions he leapt.

The drops bright love wept, shall they never be fading?
No, never; nor Octobers rain down, not reminding.

What colors the memory? What reddens the fruit.
What washes it new? What silvers a roof.

Who see in the raindarks the dread legends crying,
Who hear through the chinks—go you, keep, then, in hiding.

With the spring of a lion, heart, dark still, you leap.
Why does no deep red of Wisdom's fruit keep?

1. The legend of Pyramus and Thisbe, who stabbed themselves by the mulberry, resembles the story of Romeo and Juliet.

30

SONG FOR A RESPITE

Turn your river-dark eyes to the fields of promise.
Hear the once pipered fifes skirling gay under hills.
Let the oaks in the forest be the tall dead heroes
And your terrible longings, the mist as it sails.

Lay down the arrows. Aside, now! Pluck strings that are finer.
Say, say what the meadowwinds sang through your hair.
Pursuing the wild boars of dreams you run harder O lover
The dust-clouds blind. Now, with song, clear the air.

Put your heart like the bucket to the cut maple.
Let your blood run as sweet, gather deep to the dream.
Let the moon throw its spear and the shaft of Saint Michael
Floodlight the ghost-cluttered passageways of the brain.

They are cluttered with conjured O conjured sorrows,
Good for trapping the dust. Know, love, nothing dies but the flesh.
Let the lost heroes secretly called ring this forest
And song break forth from the love you thought dead.

If the thicket you thrash is your heart twisting twisting
See the lion stride by, grace itself, unalarmed.
Leave thorn-fences to lackloves; stretch your arms free this evening.
Time, like the lion let stride by, is Time charmed.

Night closes the woodlilies. Let it so close the eyelids.
From crown down to sole feel the fevers, lo! falling.
O first and last tale learning over and over ever
If dusk lead to dark then is dawning dawning

IV   *ARMS AND THE MAN*

AENEAS

*. . . and turning around, he found his beloved lost in
the ruins of the town.*   AENEID, BOOK II

Creüsa, cried for, through the tomb of Troy
When the bright town changed like a May dandelion
Her golden dome turned powder gray;

Creüsa, cried for; with stumbling step,
Eyes as if slapped, in his great quick loss,
Aeneas, retracing the empty streets, said
As we too once said, that it could not be thus;

Only to scatter his hope like the down
Of a gray May dandelion.
And since, after leaving behind spring and home,
I have known the small golden hopes change so,
I wonder how he could still turn to show
All those men their tired way.
O round bright dome that was blown gray.

❦ ACHILLES

I blame it on an epic,
Reading that tumultuous book:
Achilles raged into his tent,
Sent legions spinning like toy tops;
Dogged Agamemnon firm, he rants
With all his love's importunance.

I blamed it on an epic
That, thrown with his wrath,
My pulse was a hoof
Routing grass,
Kicking wishes. The whole world,
Vain dust around me, choked.

I blame it on an epic
Refusing to whimsey with a world
Always blighting loves we cherish.
I'll hold unbending sword,
For small betrayals make great falter.
I'll keep in my own camp
As he, when Agamemnon took
From him, Achilles' Trojan maid,
Achilles' sweetest Trojan maid.

Sit there then, brave one,
Your half-moon mouth curved down,
Sulk and press your weight into the chair,
Make it bear the crease where sat a lord
Thinking of Achilles in his tent.
But unlike him no brass-clad legions care
Whether you love or spite,
Whether you spoil or create.
Though you speak the truth
It won't make their sun blaze brighter,
And all there is to say is trite,
And if you swear, or sing out prayer,
O mouth strangely curved,
You are, in grief, to all but one, absurd;
You are to all but one, as unobserved.
And if you draw forth pen or sword
To right the day with all your worth,
It's but to know
The only one who cares is the King Himself.

Don't tell me how the tower stood
A thousand lives ago or why
The battlemented palace should
Stand in reflective eye.
There is the place and we can walk
As once they walked, men undismayed
By story, pleased by shape and brick,
When death and battle had not made
Its glory; let me take
In stride the tower,
                  and the friend,
Before hearing fable or fact.
For where are friends but in eyes that tell
How the hand might take the hand,
And if it's said that he would sell
At price of devil, understand.
    O would it change the glance, or range
    The step between who are not strange?

Trieste

TULIP SONG   *St. Stephen's Green, Dublin*

For Brendan Behan

Stroll away, heart, from these tulips grown tall;
Soon the huge petals slowly collapse as
Arms of loved mothers to their sides fall
Gently resigned to the last.

Nor let the two-fisted hopes unfold; see
The leaves of gold summer itself trampled, swept
Ditchwards in times that are cold. O lonely
Stand who'd risk all for the dream once dreamt.

Let grow the dread roots born in the dark days
Deep, till a loving sun charge with leaves,
Knowing the love that braves loss waves more bravely as
Out of the prison of cold, trees shoot green.

But Easters hear the lost guns of light charge
And stir with their *GLORIAS* your godly mistrust:
Tulips loaded with color grow large
While the smuggled guns grow rust . . .

So stroll away, seer, beyond rising buds
Into dim places, remembering the bards
Sang best in cells darkest; in dusty pub
Sing your love so, because, seeing far:
 Tulips, watered by rebels' blood,
 From the earth of their too vivid dreaming sprung,
 Tell to the dreamer of never-dead love;
 Tulips tell of the never-dead love.

EPITAPH FOR A RECUSANT GRAVE

We were quick for our faith to fight but our fate was to fall.
We must follow the only way we know huge and high.
Let the streams of Heaven run red! we have not lost.
You who battle the Darkness, remember the breath of our lives:
    Whosoever dies for Love does never die.

The storks are white and grace the chapel towers;
Bulls stand big and black; we muse again—
Wildlife does not change. The palace glowers
Over the dry and hot and yellow plain.

This land is but a slightly more lost land,
Shooting the fireworks tonight because Might conquered.
The saints look sideways; the Indignant band
In secret cellars to protest Love suffers.

Alive and buried, there are those who were
Extreme, as heaven and hell must be extreme;
Who could be cruel, as history is cruel;
Who clashed like gladiators in the ring.

Amongst cab-drivers, clerks, and café sitters,
I walk. What happens to a revolution?
Can lines around the mouth betray the sinners?
The face of Spain stares back, avoiding question,

Diverts our thought to storks about the court,
Where stone was set to stone with poverty's blood.
It's not a land I probe, but shape of heart:
Is Evil such a tougher mate than Good?

Believers are consumed by their belief,
A revolution by its rabid gods;
Who must concern his heart knows no relief
For love must always play against the odds.

And now in Spain the pendulum is stopped.
In rigid eyes the residue of hate
Shows terror leaves a wound not quick to clot.
The diplomats? They arrive correctly late.

Winter, and the swarthy look of noon.
Later, when the sun came out, a wind
Swept down through the ditches in my head;
The hills stood in the sun, the air was wine,
And I walked out a moment towards the woods
Before the hour faded at my back.

The roadways of the morning lay in mud;
But farther on, the world was blue and white!
And in the armpits of an oak I saw
In copper-colored leaves the deathbed's wish.
Huntsmen disappeared between the trees,
And all the hemlocks stood, confronting me.

Hunters, men who knew what thing they sought,
Struck my envy. Action simplifies.
The hilltops cried for climbers; I would climb,
Would climb till torn, had they not stopped me there,
The copper leaves that left me vaguely sad,
The brittle laugh of oak-leaves in my ears—

Visions meant for old remembering men,
Or children, faces pressed at windowpane.
Another one could take the tender day
That freshened him and neatly drink it up.
I handled all the joy of crisp cold woods
Like rarest porcelain shattering mortal touch.

Not more in woods than towns is freedom free:
The drinking-songs, the conversations, clocks
Babbled on beneath the frozen creek.
The footprints freeze upon the frightened heart.
Hollows whistled; hills were growing black;
Lamps lit, and, empty-handed, I walked back.

In the long-agos I was christened in creeks.
Eyes of violets, frogs, wild nuts,
Bend, O bend you your light once more on me
That my mind's eye may breach unbreachable gulfs.
    Log sleek with moss, ancient leaves no wind blew,
    The gay ghostly lands seen in hoof-print of deer:
    Realm where the eyes reign: here, to see is to do;
    But the creek flows so gently I should not be here.

Hush! or the grass and the turtledove
Are cast in the oven. A small wing soars:
It is mine, recovering a corner no devils love—
Immemorial moments by the muddy floors.
    As when in the death-still center of his gale
    Chardin observed how a plum took the light,
    I would store up such love, till all the colors pale
    And the bracken about my limbs grow tight.

Beetle, watercress, sweet moist earth:
Bitter days in dark cities still stare from a ditch,
But the light from a running creek, snatched from the mouth
Of time, can lend me the heart of a witch.
    On a broomstick of light my vision shall ride:
    Jump, creek! talk, minnow! cling, hair, to burr!
    At heel, nostalgia! Lost joy at my side
    Walking with me by the muddy creeks, be my heart's spur!

For the Hungarian Rebels

Gray dogs howl for the rebel dead
In the darkening hills beyond the towns.
Their echoes gather in my head
As colors in the sky fall down,
And windows blacken that reflected red.

Down the hooded streets I pray
We'll get where thoughts have wished to go;
And feelings, fearings, block the way
Like flocks of sheep on dusky roads.
Guns are booming while we pray.

But see now tall in the glowing west
A smokestack dreams of Athens' blue.
Eyes of alleycats reflect
Lost sacred sands their Egypts knew,
And those lands spreading in my breast.

In shadow now the lanes grow still
As rooms when someone speaks the truth,
As when the crowds left God's red hill,
Hill rising like that moon in the south;
And all the volcanoes threatening to spill.

And Dante and tall Virgil glide
Gesturing scorn across the breeze;
The body of the day would stride
O toward them now, but falls on its knees:
Somewhere the afternoon had lied.

On dark frontiers new troops invade,
Invade while our terror holds its breath,
Wondering how can the play be played
While the stars, all, point to death,
To powder-kegs, and prayers not prayed.

But think the moon in its brightening shows
That the eye of Heaven, loving, looks
As turning into the dusk we go
Away from the vaudeville. The books
Pressing blood-stained petal, close.

At breakfast-time there is a pond
Where blossoms an ideal; we reach;
Before our hands does it now drown?
O hear who ask You now: Look now
To them, Lord; look from that cloud's breach;
Say those were Your howling hounds!

❧ REBELLION

Budapest—New York, December 1956

Dust in the fog dropped opal, and down the East River
Night setting fire to the bridges would drown what we knew:
Out over the halls ringing eloquence taller rose the horror;
Budapest, from between the stars, stared warning what dreams can do.

The bridges, all, burning before us; the world to cross embers—
O the gay wines, could they hush, now, the jackboots of time?
We walked in the light of stars spinning to death. December
Flung in the face of each dream each dawn a new crime.

But that day would die in its flame, like the moth blind to terror.
How else, when to think with one's blood leaves other ways vain?
Heart, heart: none so darkened would follow his darkener forever,
High deeds downthundering like hoofs when fire sweeps a plain.

§

New York, from a height, hell-bright . . . why my elation
When it seemed there Nineveh smouldered and nothing could last?
Golden cities had been buried before, by an angry discussion.
I saw them stand, tall in the eyes, as they quoted kings past;

And called the lost village when pinetree-lights sparkled Park Avenue:
Child, Child born in squalor, be born where those torn streets burn!
And here, cast away the false thrones I see newly glitter
Watching us play the death-games no century's love learned . . .

Cairo, and Damascus—and Sennacherib rising in the shadows.
On the islands, in Cyprus, Antigone on trial at noon.
The witches of the East in a double sense paltering ever—
And in Budapest the stone rolls to, sealing the tomb.

§

And slowly as December smoked up between the rivers
The ghost of a Robespierre shuffled across the skies.

46

It twisted the treaties like the last plane-leaves, scraps for no beggar;
It turned the dream to a nightmare of blood and flies.

It tore the flag of the Magyar, waved the rag at Heaven.
But the woods were moving, moving; Tomorrow, a Dunsinane;
Though time like the curtain sever Today from Tomorrow—
That face in the ruins, the soul, was peering through the flames!

§

And walking from the galleries of Central Park, seeking a picture,
I thought of far places still left: Corot's willowed Spring,
How Goya had painted despair in another cruel hour;
I thought of the only palace no troop could storm;

Thought of those who changed the wine into blood with a vision
Following forever a way that was huge and high,
Draining that cup of agony, as this hour's patriot:
Petoëfi walked forth to die.

§

And if jackboots trampled, trembled each meadow an Aetna,
Deafening the cry of the dying rebel, and our shame,
If the leaves, all, were twisted, still among the branches
The bleeding trees held high the night, in all its pain.

Because Lose is Save, however the day nail the dream.
It's the slaughtered Lamb, O loved land as that Lamb outpoured.
No streets glittered hell as from a height this moment seemed,
Though the legions bear weapons not dreamt of before.

§

But taking madness as the ant with care confounding the cobra,
The terrible prayer of the saint singing through Dark Night,
The rebel's hand tearing at the tanks—kindled by fury,

47

Will be driven that unholy ghost, from sight.

For the sword dangling over the dream shall quicken the dreamer.
If winds from the steppes sweep blood to the steppes of our sleep,
Let the night of pain change the wine of dreams to life blood.
Budapest: since that first Easter there is no defeat!

§

What captured Corot's spring willow, but the fair hour's impermanence?
But they sang, on the way to a Bastille, with their full breath.
What charges the day with high deed but tragedy's imminence.
Heart: wise with life, those foolish deaths shall fool Death!

As metropolitan riverwinds rushed me along I remember
The beaded eyes of the streets wheeled like terrible toys;
And all the stars in the field of night downpiercing—
All those, too, they were also turning to terrible toys.

Star, star: they are saying you are only a dangerous toy.
Moon: they are daring you down the sky!
O Moon, more beautiful now as more perilous:
Why have you let them infringe on your lonely pride?

J. F. K.

Ireland, June 26, 1963

Strange turn of fate that brings him back again
To this loved land his forbears left in pain:
    From Famine, the Phoenix rises: he, to the age
    Leading to mend a torn dark century's page.

    O Fathers long-ago oppressed:
    Here is a fruit from all your tragic past:
One ruined island, small and poor, sent forth
One man to wrest rich worlds from ruined earth.

Great turn of fate . . .

§

November 22, 1963

As if, as if
Too great,
That turn.
Against the God,
Strange gods have won.
And that's not strange:
He, loved, dies young.
Who only came to lead
Became
The very Heart of Day,
Became
The True Prince of the Age.
O
Forbid the bitter iron
Entering the soul:
That he, too, he,
Huger than fate,
Must go, so;
Must
Go the way men go when great.

V ARMS DIVINE

THE BODY IS A DIVINING ROD

Cottonwood towering, pollendown snowing in the sun;
Broken fences, and beyond, meadow vibrant with dock:
Sweet Ghost I had else thought delusion, I saw how You
Open the Elysium gates no hand unlocks.

Watched nothing but streams over pebbles all that summer.
Fool! to be following wet light . . . O hazel-rod,
I grew to know to idle so, thought-quiet, eye-wide, were
Not straying by oneself but betraying one's Self to one's God.

Secret light sending arms out, face down, pull in limb, Flesh at odds—
Surrendering to unending hidden waters of gold: end of wandering was
To begin bending bodily to deeps, as divining-twigs nod,
Begging body bend ever to the dark streams of gold, of God!

I awoke this morning to a world snowing wonders,
Throwing flakes of delight over every bleak twig,
And the daybreak, blue, flooding the windows as thunder
Spells dumb; and streetlamps like chandeliers lit.
Snowy every sprig, pebble, brown reed—snowladen;
I looked to the white-shouldered sky: swathed in lace!
Saw a telegraph-wire because it went straight
But couldn't have told it from tree-limb's grace
Except for the line . . .

                O disguise so our fate! O
Snow falling down on our days near the Day
Disguise with white wishes our days in the face
Of Noel, as its Child sees nor richrobes nor rags
But, as snowy day, knows not the rosebed from sands,
But covers with love, like a snowy sky, all.

And the sun walking over the trees like a bride
And the trailings of rice-throwing snowclouds, and high
Beaded pools in the woodlands were brimming champagnes.
Sun sent the blue shadows bright through the brain.
Was the world white and gold? It was new, that cold breeze.
Then arise from the sheets and go over sleet fields
To marry the day, for a day. Pledge be sealed.

❦ PETRARCH FOR LAURA

To my mother

Morninglight around her like a sash of glory—
Pools in the wood, till she look, search blank sky.
Phlox glowing white from the gardendarks
Of deep summernights are in her eye.

I would trade all the branches of spring for her gesture;
It plucks the chord stirring Thought from the lair.
Columbine lifting the gloom are her fingers—
Silent bells ringing the air,

As forests brood till bright of bloodroot;
The brain awakens to her April face.
Her voice is the coming upon real water in a desert,
Gardens of phantasy ablossom in her train,

Where Time is but a sundial's design, circling all the proverbs—
The ancient stone gods remembering the dawns on their isles;
Mercury in flight, and the sound of silver fountains
Taking the clay from wit's wing is her smile.

Then wood-throats, tell the blue hills to echo
Through whom simple song becomes praise:
She send the ragged rhymes into vision rising regal,
Holy festivals tolling when she strolls through a common day.

✿✿ INTOXICATION

For Henri Peyre

Il faut être toujours ivre. BAUDELAIRE

In an orchard abandoned I sing, wild with scent of apple;
A hunter's dusk reddens; the thunder of musketry quakes;
Pheasants start; apples drop; the Earth speaks: This matters:
To live in the wilderness of a vision, keen as deer at the brake;

To rise to that romance like pheasant from dark hunt is
To breathe in a drink more quickening than cognac,
To taste of a dawn-fragrance welled for Eve's gladness—
Drop pure as dew: it's with this, Love has wished to be drunk, as

A lord; as explorer come to gold climes;
As youth running romany roads to the sun:
We thirst for fruit of some knowledge sublime—
And a drop of wild truth in the head leaves us drunk,

When the very Wilderness sings, urging answer:
I, to say this: One thing, more than all else, matters:
The spirit that reaches, and reaches, for the Unknown Drop,
Touching depths to find heights to drink of the tears of the God.

Albany, Vermont

She arose at the screech of dawn, with the gabble of geese
And the glory of desolate creatures warming her eye;
Changed a lowly farm to a realm, though few worldlings see,
For we've shut out the light that hallows grey silo, great scythe;
But she who spent years in famed cities was not by them waylaid;
Nigh lowing cattle I heard the Cloud's voice toll the sky;
Spider-strung windows hung histories to shame sash of empire;
In the dust were motes plucked from the blind eye of temporal time.
So: it found me there—now sounding my very brain—the mystery of the manger.

§

Bathed as christened in that river, Black River, of ghostly north beauty,
And the blue vigin woodstream lit cistern like dreamt wishes,—sent.
Realm grounded in her learning of poets and the poetry of tubers . . .
In her terrible wayward quest
Youth towered into its truest heritage, because
We shall be wise as the ground we know grow, rich as lands within eye.
In a stone's glint I gleamed early Greece, strolled foothills of oracle,
Saw Rome in its ruins for needing these pure sweeping skies;
Knew all the Fruits of the Gods—in our hands! if soul like soil we but toil.

§

And she, lighting kindling, like a Pharaoh's strayed queen—herself the fire;
Nor knowing, or how heart were sowing her bitter-sweet truths;
Slow, they grow; deep; I reap: O Majesty, meshed in a mire!
Heart weeds out dark loves and the Leaves of the God see to climb.
So, goldenrod-sceptre: fall from the dreaming child's fingers:
My head rapt, mind-blind, in fantastical cloud-castles of youth—
Till I profaned her brave love like the True Rose that crowns with Death's briar;
Bleed, dreams; die! that the Kingdom Come can come down into mind:
    Cattle-trough cradle: reborn, there, is Love's only story:
    As she changed a stark farm to a realm enriching mind's eye,
    As, once, changed a dark manger to the Cradle of the Age's Glory,
    So: Kingdom, come! change O my dark human love—to Divine!

❦ THE HONEY LOCUST TREE[1]

Grand River, Michigan

That August when the river broad-brimming rushed Indian,
I fell along the banks tugging to me those horizons,
To breathe the far age that spiked height to pine,
Hunting Grounds Happy behind them to find,
On a noon tangled deep in wild-parsley, lone weedy
Impossible knowledge ablossom . . .

                    Where every field
Exploded gold fern, fell, my mammon, sated;
All shelter to be wished, it was there! above, leaf-layered:
The best bed a bankslope with but a gnarled root
Of oak between the Lethe there (final loving) and foot,
Yet drowning in the twisty waves of tall grasses,
As certain as in current, should limbs, challenged, chance in.

    Yarrow I crushed sent Time deep breathing,
Breathed awake ancient days Today dimmed from me, lost to me—
The pungent-wrung air rang with discovery.
O sweet wild twist:

                  so! does soul wake from body,
Does sighting, grief-wrung, sweep alive, stinging air;
Bruised, thinking steals young, bold as huntsman to lair—
Till pulled as by arms, from vision I clambered,
Rescued from thought, declaring war, wardanced
    Till the stonydust kicked stories of fire,
    Till the pink of dusk bled, and refreshed, muscle tired—
    The weights of the flesh, loosening, dropped as to seafloors,
    Released, lost as paths dimming into the marshfields,
And singing as in danger, in glory, till breath-robbed,
I leaned against a tree. O sharp!

                  What was this thorned bark?
This wood encircled with, as midnight bright, tall as rain,
As sunrise eye-widening, as by sundowns stained:

1. The honey locust tree grows large thorns around its bole.

60

Branchings duskily climbing as
Cloud like the loaded rose, blown, outlined them;
   Huge grew their secret, as moon when sky blackens:
   Not branches now, but bayonets, brandished;
To what were these death-dealing weapons pointing?
And I looked as to lightning: "Not strike!" let no voice say.
But prised eye, saw then:
                     O Crown, Crown! I cried,
This is the tree, this the tree, by my side.
   Within my grasp grew what stabbed
   The man, the Man, the Son of Man.
      Heart: beat may you now, or let all beating stop:
      This do you see, the headgear of God.

   §

Broken, the dome of that dusk, like the Bread.
Like storm through blossoming fruittrees it spread
The sorrowing joy of the earth to the earth,
Squandering brightness to the fields of night. Burst
First-last break of the vaguely aching heart:
The air of two thousand years ago was in my throat—
That very air within the lung.
Locust, Honey Locust, destroying the dust,
All loot
In one shoot:
I unscabbered the Sword of the World where I tore a thin sprig;
The crown of the King dug my flesh where I clutched a black twig.

   §

Not under lock and key framed in relic gold way, not
Lodged in casket of ancient queen nor buried in catacomb's vault.
No, but growing in the wind on an Indian riverbank,
Lonely.

Tossed from me, lost was that
Happy Ground's hunting, found wound around the Locust.
Stood there all the sky rang *SANCTUS*,
SANCTUS . . .
                    The sun's last light
Thrice struck the breast of that riverbank's night,
Trees there towered cloaked in black
As those who came to bless this savage grass,
Raise holy the head. Heroic all
Those trees told how Loyola stood tall,
Jean de Brébeuf, Isaac Jogues . . .
Around that bole
The crowns they wore as they praising died,
Chanting, no requiem but the soughing of the pines.
Coming armed with thunder not of musket but crucifix,
Lightening heathen night as my sight by that instant is.

      §

And the old Indian river ran wine and fire;
Within its swollen waters flowed the veins of that desire,
All Here can know of the lengths, depths, of Love.
Dusklit, the reddening eddies rushed
Regal the river a road to that throne
Overhead, and through my head said: Never this let go unknown,
This, this shown.
    Beam by the motes of that broad-brimming river,
    Tree you had changed the vain vision: the waters
    Of the world run wine become holy; and only
    Who could bleed for that Word tell how live who love wholly.
After that drop, Flesh and Blood walks the dream.
After that drop, Found is what was Seek.

§

Carry, then, in, through, and out of the night,
The sight of it stinging to sing away fright.
 The Ghost that howls round the bends of the chest wears that thorn.
 The Ghost that calls from the depths never-dead bears that sword.
O blood, be quickened by that sound as hounds by the horn.
Let spread your sound through the head, as through wood hunter's horn!

Strolling from libraries and fountains, tall with lore, learning, legend—
Poplarleaves twisting, reflecting the charge of his talk
Drawing, as rains stud the dust, the lost ages to crystal;
The centuries around him like spreading lawns green with his wit;

From courtyards and cloisters forgotten where queens fled to prayer—
(O father, "when the waters creep in, even unto the breast . . . ")
But the tragic robes rustle quick, alive in your shadow:
You step setting pebbles astir with history's trysts;

Step hovering on the rims of my visions as towering the rooftops
That dome of St. Peter's; condemn then, approve them, like Rome.
Whose compass is in your head that you cut through forest
As the first early fathers, unfalteringly toward the lost home?

And the poplarleaves flashing to my mind that silver, green palace
As thoughtful you walk, springing cool from your own spreading flames.
Loneliness packed bright in the head like the snow on the mountains;
The shoulder pulled by the ancient gael young in your veins.

§

Crows, flap away! plants, fold him! who comes will be plucking
The bleeding foot, bleeding yet, but it's out of the snare.
Stay, stay, red deer, nor fear this step; breathe deep; listen:
Heaths blue with unknown grasses blow past his hair.

And the windy moon never letting him alone, never blackened—
It is spilled on his head; it's the wash of that moon in his eye,
Breasting a faint-hearted world as in a gray evening
Moon grows brave, drawing the small waves high.

Circling what purgatorios, refusing excuses,
Refusing himself excuses to soothe away thought.
But the crows caw away from the darkened one's brooding:
His eyes say the white wings of wish, deeply sought, shall downflock.

Squandering those gentle ways reviving like hyssop,
Striking spark from stone; and the blackened watchfires leap.
Whose divining rod is his arm? It's the subtlety of plants in his fingers
Folding in light, and unfolding to the planets of his thought.

§

But too tall to salute. It is Michael descends in his footfall;
May those ghosts so haunt me then, till Lost be Won.
Till no day but remembers what remembered they to my father:
Every child is the child of a King.

❧ *REQUIEM*

Pius XII, October 9, 1958

Silvermaples filled with sunrise, sweeping heap on smouldering heap
Leap to him from the bonfires circling blue the country lanes;

Winds that bruise sad ditches gay—they know for whom gold censers heave;
Lanes in ashes, all, wing fair what David and the Sibyl say.

§

Crimsoned hawthorn decks the casket; pall of red silk spreading shrub—
Clear to all tint, all scent, is how and why he left this day.

Alchemies astir the earth, stir deeper now, to praise the Dove:
Leaves released from trees flare gold, show death to earth goes radiant, gay.

§

O Dove that passed, in words he did, from bend of thought to send of limb,
He spoke, he blessed, all movement had, as could at wish ascend.

Who hold the Key unlock all joy, all sorrow lock. The call is his:
"ALLEVIATE MY GRIEF!" he could, and labouring, stayed instead.

§

Tongues of fire sweep the leaves as all his thought the Tongue above.
South of Rome last week, allwheres he stands as choirs chant.

DIES IRAE, echoing through the oakgrove, gilds the rust;
Elms that last week tan leaf dangled guard this dawn, tall, black.

§

DIES ILLA, echoing, sets the lichened bark aglow;
O lichen like that grief-chant blacking silver though the night;

Low tones like that blue-green mould not hoar, but luminous grow,
Throwing where the ground most dark is—light!

66

§

Deep in the wood a waterpool shot back the dusk;
They were blessing the bier; and the pool brimmed sacred with his gaze—

ABSOLVE: *ABSOLVE*: the last swallows splashed, the deer knelt
And the haze tracing over the meadows of dawn veiled his face.

§

Wildcarrot, goldenrod rusting the grasses—withered this day closed.
Thistles bursting purple brilliance, and the witch-hazel shrub shot aspark

Lone flame the fading meadows: they are gathering in purple and gold.
Last woodland asters thread the fields with centuried noble garb.

§

KYRIE ELÉISON sweeping the maplewood, the lifting boughs hung with
    its notes;
CHRISTE ELÉISON falling, downfloating the leaves tumbling gold to lawn:

Those—the tones in the windy boughs, sending them tall, bending low,
And the voice at the heart of the grove grown grave in the dawn.

§

Great ash covert ablaze tells how rays filtered down Rome's dome
And catching on that mitre of the sun described all height.

Black-willows flashing silver insideout—the armour shone
As breastplates in the basilica flashed lost ages back in sight.

§

Brown leaves down the paths steep piling tell how aisles file deep
As they shuffle, muffled, out into the emptied evening air

There where the evening-star tells how he followed toiling late;
It guided him, as once three kings, till farthest Far was Here.

67

§

October tolling *REQUIESCAT*: oak and hemlock stretching tall;
Dropping fruit strike sorrow's note. *OREMUS* stirs the paths;

All tongues, athrong the aisles, and leaves in lanes, low murmuring, bow:
The chant of the wind through the bush is the ancient Mass.

§

From pinecone floor to hemlock height—copse, meadow, ditch, lawn, glen,
Redolent, resonant shone with the tones tolling the Death into Life.

Every wood gold weed, fern, rush, reed, fervent folded as for him;
Participants all, they celebrate, celebrate!

§

But it's summery among the formal gardens, fountains, ilex trees,
Among the lemon-blossoms no glooms wreathe I see him stroll;

That fair land where the orange blows, it is there, love, there where he walks,
And the finch on the branch of his wrist like the Holy Ghost.

§

Summery as all those overtones of joy the Requiem rang.
Raked leaves now catching rains to hasten spring, brim like the fonts;

All earth his bier; the grounds prepared, we'll see, in days of sun,
The blossoms of Tomorrow springing taller with his light.

Having squandered my years to follow that wake beyond the elm
Where cold the moon wheels carefully on unfurling cloud,
Having bartered any wit for a light not sold except, except for a song,
Staked midnights like chips on a number not there,
For a sum O where? Not here (I hear now) not here to be won—
Willing stillness stretch tight the veins that they might,
Plucked by no earthly hand, someday render true one,
One sound—
Wits as twanging away, I have this much to say: Do not stop
When the whisper among the leaves of quiet says *"LISTEN. . . !"*
Not stop.
       No: that murmur, though than green of leaf clearer,
Deeper ringing, more bitter, a mockery of eardrum,
Of iris, of tastebud . . . say O now it was perhaps but
But the burring of the heavy moths gold at the edge of the copse,
But the stirring of woodfern searching the dark night of earth.
Turn away! This say:
            this.
          Or let pressed be,
As first clustered grapes,
Let pressed be the braincells, staining all sight inside;
Pressed until body but a goatskin hold much heady wine,
Till Time like the Ice Sheet begin, melt thin,
Old legend pushed young into sun,
Frozen mystery to roll, there to lie, before the eye,
Seeming one day simple, sound, warm.
No, that tone of leaf taller than height sending where? O
Had but for barter, all bartered,
And freely (only) given, as April air, but for the breathing,
Giving all, given all,
Will take every once-shed salt tear in the chest,
Will break every not-yet-shed tear in the head,
And drink those drops, all, with one sip, imperceptible sip.

§

Go. Go your ways. Be not dazed. Do not praise, but in
Ageless old ways
Like the waves of the sea, salt or grass, that repeat,
Sweet repeat.
For walking the wood, what do I see but unfoldings
Each moment more strange,
Tricking the lane, the brain, and the pain:
Weeds live as beasts and never the same
Expression gestured from bough.
A spruce growing bluer in the rain saying "Gaze! Graze, love, now!
Now give tongue to my wonder numb ways, for tomorrow is never."
It taught me, it tossed me my thought (fallen cone,
And all thought a slow falling to the floors, lying low
Like those cones . . .)
Taught: quiet as a pinecone in shade I might learn how to praise.
As still as a stone in a valley I might learn firm praise.
But stop, stilled by growths in a woodlight, and crazed
The fool brain shall fool dervish and downdrop.
Stand sighting the woodlily that tells not to toil—
But, Lord, not to toil is to coil unto death
Unless unless like the cobra clever
Love roll away like old skin.

§

Do not, I advise you, my charming ambitions in a heap
As robes after revelry and the wine-flasks dry, do not pray
But gay sing away, gay and loud sing the night blue to dawn.
Forget the one crown to be wished is won for the willing.
Nor think to catch sound of the only Voice. Nor follow
That streak in the sky:
It belongs to the Grail, and you will, unaware,
All failing, succeed like the day-
Break of day, break of once black heart.
And the once wooden twigs leasing tears, tossing pearls, dropping

70

Rain on the head become chrism—
What return can the beggar brain render but in shedding of blood?
What give but that wish: To shed its loved blood?

And that Grail: before the very eye—it is there!
Waiting, waiting, waiting
Only to be seen and followed.
But not; do not alter your pauper-proud dusty steps.
Do not believe it. Fool-happy sleepwalker, No!
Sleep, sleep, sleep.

A NOTE ON THE TYPE

The text of this book has been set on the Monotype in a typeface named *Bell*. Monotype Bell is a facsimile version of the letter cut in 1788 by Richard Austin for John Bell's British Letter Foundry. Some fonts of Bell, the first British modern face, were purchased in 1864 by Henry O. Houghton for his Riverside Press in Cambridge, Massachusetts, and these types were listed as "English Copperface" in the 1887 specimen book of the Press. Some books and pamphlets were printed from these types for Martin Brimmer of Boston, but afterwards the types lay dormant for many years until they were "rediscovered" by Bruce Rogers in 1898 and, under the name Brimmer, used in many distinguished books designed by him. Some fonts of Bell were acquired in 1903 by Daniel Berkeley Updike for his Merrymount Press and used there under the name Mountjoye. Since that time, researches by Stanley Morison have shown that Brimmer, Mountjoye, and Bell are one and the same. This monotype cutting was done in 1931 from punches now in the Stephenson, Blake foundry.

This book was designed, composed, and printed by
Clarke & Way at the Thistle Press, New York.
Bound by H. Wolff, New York.